Loved & Lost
You Will Always Be Remembered

Loved & Lost
You Will Always Be Remembered

Loved & Lost
You Will Always Be Remembered

Letters to Those Loved & Lost:
You Will Always Be Remembered

Loved & Lost
You Will Always Be Remembered

Loved & Lost
You Will Always Be Remembered

Letters to Those Loved & Lost:
You Will Always Be Remembered
~Lena Ma

© 2020

Loved & Lost
You Will Always Be Remembered

Loved & Lost
You Will Always Be Remembered

MAD GIRL'S LOVE SONG

I shut my eyes and all the world drops dead;
I lift my lids and all is born again.
(I think I made you up inside my head.)

The stars go waltzing out in blue and red,
and arbitrary blackness gallops in:
I shut my eyes and all the world drops dead.

I dreamed that you bewitched me into bed
and sung me moon-struck, kissed me quite insane.

(I think I made you up inside my head.)

God topples from the sky, hell's fires fade:
exit seraphim and Satan's men:

I shut my eyes and all the world drops dead.

I fancied you'd return the way you said,
but I grow old and I forget your name.
(I think I made you up inside my head.)

Loved & Lost
You Will Always Be Remembered

I should have loved a thunderbird instead;
at least when spring comes they roar back again.

I shut my eyes and all the world drops dead.
(I think I made you up inside my head.)

- Sylvia Plath

Loved & Lost
You Will Always Be Remembered

Loved & Lost
You Will Always Be Remembered

Loved & Lost
You Will Always Be Remembered

TABLE OF CONTENTS

Prologue
16

Chapter One
A Letter To My First Crush:
You Are The Reason I Am Capable Of Love
19

Chapter Two
A Letter To The One Who Keeps Fucking With My Head:
You Are The Reason I Have Self-Doubt
24

Chapter Three
A Letter To The Love I Made Up Out Of Loneliness:
You Are The Reason I Am Fucked Up
29

Chapter Four
A Letter To The One I Rejected And Regretted:
You Are The Reason I Am Self-Destructive
34

Loved & Lost
You Will Always Be Remembered

Chapter Five
A Letter To The Hand Who Slaps Me Across The Face:
You Are The Reason I Run From My Past

39

Chapter Six
A Letter To My First Intimate Love:
You Are The Reason I Possess Anger And Rage

44

Chapter Seven
A Letter To The One I Meet Under Lockdown:
You Are The Reason I Am No Longer Logical

49

Chapter Eight
A Letter To The One Who Takes Advantage Of Me:
You Are The Reason I Remain Silent

54

Chapter Nine
A Letter To My Longest, Yet Most Toxic, Relationship:
You Are The Reason I Am Traumatized

59

Chapter Ten
A Letter To The Unexpected And Shallow Breakup:
You Are The Reason I Despise Men

65

Loved & Lost
You Will Always Be Remembered

Chapter Eleven
A Letter To The One I Left Unexpectedly:
You Are The Reason I Deserve To Be Ghosted

70

Chapter Twelve
A Letter To The One Who Could Have Been:
You Are The Reason I Have No Standards

74

Chapter Thirteen
A Letter To The One Who Fell For All My Bullshit:
You Are The Reason I Have No Shame

79

Chapter Fourteen
A Letter To The One Who Refuses To Stop:
You Are The Reason I Fear Others

84

Chapter Fifteen
A Letter To The One Who Ghosted Me:
I Deserve It.
Karma Does Exist.

89

Loved & Lost
You Will Always Be Remembered

Chapter Sixteen
A Letter To The One Who Calls Me A Freak For Being Myself:
You Are The Reason I Pretend To Be Someone I'm Not

93

Chapter Seventeen
A Letter To The One Who Lured Me In With No Intention Of Keeping Me:
You Are The Reason I Question My Judgments

98

Chapter Eighteen
A Letter To The One Who Thinks I Will Never Be Good Enough:
You Are The Reason I Turn Against Myself

103

Chapter Nineteen
A Letter To The Love I Have Found:
Will You Leave Too?
Or Will My Pattern Of Unfortunate Relationships Finally Come To An End?

108

Chapter Twenty
A Letter To The Person I Have Neglected My Entire Life:
You Are My One True Love, And I Will Never Leave You Again

113

Loved & Lost
You Will Always Be Remembered

Epilogue
118

Loved & Lost
You Will Always Be Remembered

PROLOGUE

Love.

When it is right, it can be a beautiful thing.
However, when it is not, it can create destruction far beyond our imaginations.
Love can be innocent.
Love sends shivers down our spines and makes us feel as if we are floating.
Love gives us gifts and comfort, and it makes us never want to let go of the source it is coming from.

Loved & Lost
You Will Always Be Remembered

However, love can also be deadly.
Love can suck us in and spit us out dry.
Love can become obsessive and evil.

Love can manipulate us into doing unspeakable acts that we feel we cannot control.
Love can force us to become so narrow-minded that nothing and no one else matters.
Love can only be innocent or deadly if we allow it.
Love is an empty vessel.

Love absorbs the energy and emotions we put inside it rather than acting as a force that controls our minds.
Love can be changed.
Love has changed.

Haven't you ever been in romantic relationships, where one minute you feel as if you're floating, and the next, you feel as if you were a puppet?
Haven't you ever been in romantic relationships, where you just wanted to get out, but feel like you cannot?
Haven't you ever been in romantic relationships, where you turn from being madly in love to having complete resentment toward your partner?
This is what love does to us.

Love is so overpowering and so overwhelming that it makes us doubt and resent even ourselves.

Loved & Lost
You Will Always Be Remembered

Love can change the way we see ourselves and the world so drastically that sometimes we cannot revert.
Love makes us see the world differently depending on which side we are on.

Love makes us feel as if we are being controlled.
Are we though?

Loved & Lost
You Will Always Be Remembered

CHAPTER ONE

A Letter To My First Crush:
You Are The Reason I Am Capable Of Love

I am a young girl.
Six.
Shy.
Afraid.
Unlovable.

Then I see you.

Loved & Lost
You Will Always Be Remembered

You are perfect.
Everyone loves you.
I love you.
But you don't notice me.

Then one day, that all changes.
When you turn my life around.
You give me a card.
Teddy bears.
Hugging.
In love.
Like you and me.
The card means you love me back.
Right?

I wait.
And wait.
And wait.
And wait.
For eight years.
You pretend like you do not notice me.
Was the card meant for someone else?

Was the card just a card?
Do you even know who I am?
Do you even know my name?
Do you see the way I look at you?

Day after day, I see other girls flirting with you.

Loved & Lost
You Will Always Be Remembered

Year after year, I watch you date my friends and enemies while leaving me behind.
Do you not notice how I always make an effort to sit next to you?
Do you not notice how I treat you above everyone else?

To me, that card made me find love.
To you, that card was just a cheap card you gave to everyone.
I found love.
You are my first love.
You are my imaginary love.

Loved & Lost
You Will Always Be Remembered

Write a letter expressing your true feelings to your first crush. What do you wish you could do differently? Do not suppress. Just write.

Loved & Lost
You Will Always Be Remembered

Draw an image representing the agony of how you feel around your first crush. Do not suppress. Just draw.

Loved & Lost
You Will Always Be Remembered

CHAPTER TWO

A Letter To The One Who Keeps Fucking With My Head:
You Are The Reason I Have Self-Doubt

I see the way you look at me.
Always peeking toward my direction and hinting to hang out.
I see you.
But it's okay.
Because I like you too.

You message me funny memes, hoping they will make me smile.

Loved & Lost
You Will Always Be Remembered

They don't.
But I smile anyway.
Just for you.

I flirt with you.
You flirt back.
I flirt with you again.
You ignore me.
Wait.
What?

I don't hear from you for five days.
Then I get another meme.
I smile.
I flirt with you again.
You flirt back.
Then you leave again.
Leaving me confused.
Wondering if you ever liked me.
Or if this is all a lie.

I see you look at me one minute.
Then I see you look at someone else the next.
Are you fucking with me?
Are you playing with my head?
Back and forth.
Back and forth.
Back and forth.

Loved & Lost
You Will Always Be Remembered

You continue to mess with my mind.
I'm sorry.
I have to call it quits.
I have to block you.
I don't know what your game is, but I have to go.

Maybe I am just delusional.
Maybe you don't actually like me.
Maybe I am just being a fool.
Maybe you don't like me after all.
I'm sorry.
I have to go.

Loved & Lost
You Will Always Be Remembered

Write a letter expressing your true feelings to the one who keeps sending you mixed signals. What do you wish you could do differently? Do not suppress. Just write.

Loved & Lost
You Will Always Be Remembered

Draw an image representing the agony of how you feel when someone you like keeps screwing with your mind. Do not suppress. Just draw.

Loved & Lost
You Will Always Be Remembered

CHAPTER THREE

**A Letter To The Love I Made Up Out Of Loneliness:
You Are The Reason I Am Fucked Up**

You are my first kiss.
My first boyfriend.
My first lover.
You love me for me.

You are always around when I need you.

Loved & Lost
You Will Always Be Remembered

You stroke my hair.
You caress me.
You tell me everything will be okay as you sleep next to me at night.

Every night you remind me that I am special.
Every night you remind me that I am loved.
Every night you promise me you will never leave.
Every night you tell me you love me.

But then one day.
You disappear.
And you never come back.
Where are you?
What the hell happened?
Do you not love me anymore?
What happened to the promises you made?
I love you!
Fuck you!

Night after night, I do not hear from you.
Night after night, I cry myself to sleep.
Night after night, I wonder where you are or who you are with.
Night after night, I caress myself.
Night after night, I fall apart.

Then one night, I turn thirteen.
And I realize something.
You are not real.

Loved & Lost
You Will Always Be Remembered

You were never real.
You were only my imagination.
Created to help me cope with loneliness.
I fell in love with you when I thought I had no one.

I fell in love with you to help me deal with life.
And now you are gone.
But you will always be in my memories.
I love you.
Forever.
And ever.

Loved & Lost
You Will Always Be Remembered

Write a letter expressing your true feelings to your perfect imaginary love. What do you wish you could do differently? Do not suppress. Just write.

Loved & Lost
You Will Always Be Remembered

Draw an image representing the agony of how you feel when you are lonely. Do not suppress. Just draw.

Loved & Lost
You Will Always Be Remembered

CHAPTER FOUR

**A Letter To The One I Rejected And Regretted:
You Are The Reason I Am Self-Destructive**

You're always there.
A timid and quiet young boy.
Who always seemed like he didn't belong.
I don't really speak to you.
I don't really notice you.
You are just kind of…there.

Loved & Lost
You Will Always Be Remembered

Then one day, you reach out.
You express your feelings for me.
I laugh in your face.
I spit in your face.
My first real potential for love, and I laugh instead.
You attempt to ask me out several more times.
Time after time, I respond with distasteful humor and discontent.

You move on.
You find someone else.
You fall in love.

Two years later, I fall in love with you.
Karma's a bitch.
You are already with someone else.
You reject me.
You laugh in my face.
You spit in my face.
Karma, right?

You try being my friend.
You try not to hurt me.
But because you are with someone, that meant I do not have a place in your life or your heart.
You force yourself to detach from me.

You leave.
You come back because you don't want to actually leave.
But you get in trouble.

Loved & Lost
You Will Always Be Remembered

So, you leave again.
Each time, I fall apart.
I break.
I crumble.

I lose myself.
I fall into a pattern of self-destruction because I cannot handle unrequited love.
Karma is a bitch.
Right?

Loved & Lost
You Will Always Be Remembered

Write a letter expressing your true feelings to the love you regret leaving. What do you wish you could do differently? Do not suppress. Just write.

Loved & Lost
You Will Always Be Remembered

Draw an image representing the agony of what it feels like to walk away from potential love. Do not suppress. Just draw.

Loved & Lost
You Will Always Be Remembered

CHAPTER FIVE

**A Letter To The Hand Who Slaps Me Across The Face:
You Are The Reason I Run From My Past**

I have nothing left.
No school. No job. Just food and regret.
Vomiting. Cutting. Hating.
I feel alone.

I feel unloved.
I feel broken and defective.

Loved & Lost
You Will Always Be Remembered

I try online dating.
To distract myself from the enemy that is my mind.
I meet you.
You are charming.
You show interest in me.
You distract me from my problems.
I fall head over heels.

We talk every day.
You treat me with respect, and you help me figure out my life.
I am grateful for you.
Then you disappear.
We fade away.
We lose touch.

I never forget about you.
I always think about you whenever I feel down.
You are my angel.
You are my hand.

Five years later, we meet again.
However, this time it feels different.
You no longer act as my angel.
You no longer behave as my hand.
You are now judgmental and cold.
You now hurt me more than you help me.

You are not who I thought you were five years ago.
We felt so connected then.

Loved & Lost
You Will Always Be Remembered

So in tune.
I believed that I could count on you.

Then I meet you in person.
And all you want to do is hurt me and judge my character.
Maybe we lost touch for a reason.
Maybe we were never meant to reconnect.
This is goodbye again.
This time for real.

Loved & Lost
You Will Always Be Remembered

Write a letter expressing your true feelings to the one who betrays you. What do you wish you could do differently? Do not suppress. Just write.

Loved & Lost
You Will Always Be Remembered

Draw an image representing the agony of what it feels like to be betrayed by someone you trust. Do not suppress. Just draw.

Loved & Lost
You Will Always Be Remembered

CHAPTER SIX

A Letter To My First Intimate Love:
You Are The Reason I Possess Anger And Rage

The first few months with you feels amazing.
You keep me away from my toxic behaviors.
You treat me like a princess.
You give me everything I could possibly want.
And you never complain.
The only thing you cannot do is be honest with me.

Loved & Lost
You Will Always Be Remembered

Until it is too late.
I hear my phone go off.
And there you are.
With one of your many text messages.
This time, in the form of a break-up.
Break-up via text?
Really?

I try calling you.
You ignore me.
I continue to call you, nonstop, over the next six hours.
Your only response is another text saying we are over at hour five.

I become devastated.
I go for a walk in the park at night and cry in front of strangers.
I try and distract myself with movies only to find myself texting you.
Of all the men I have known so far, you are my first.

We started off as partners, lovers, confidants, fiancés.
Then we became enemies.
You broke my heart and sent me to be locked away.
Against my will.
Complete shutdown.
I can never forgive you.

Even when you do come back begging for forgiveness.
I no longer see you in the light I used to.

Loved & Lost
You Will Always Be Remembered

The promises we have made to each other and the love we have felt for each other no longer exist.
I do not love you anymore.

Stop calling me.
Leave me alone.
I'm done.
Asshole.

Loved & Lost
You Will Always Be Remembered

Write a letter expressing your true feelings to your first intimate love. What do you wish you could do differently? Do not suppress. Just write.

Loved & Lost
You Will Always Be Remembered

Draw an image representing the agony of what your first intimate love feels like. Do not suppress. Just draw.

Loved & Lost
You Will Always Be Remembered

CHAPTER SEVEN

**A Letter To The One I Meet Under Lockdown:
You Are The Reason I Am No Longer Logical**

I meet you in the last place I would ever want to meet someone.
In a psychiatric hospital.
I do not want to associate with anyone, but you force yourself into my life.
You take advantage of my vulnerable side and I fall in love with you.

Loved & Lost
You Will Always Be Remembered

We spend nights walking around the ward, talking about
philosophy and our future together.
You lock me in.
I discharge in bliss.

Three weeks later, you send me a letter.
A letter expressing your love for me and how you want me to be
your girlfriend.
I am excited.
I hold onto this letter.
I reach out to give you my answer.
But you do not respond.

I write a letter back and put it in your mailbox.
Yes, I stalk you.
And I find you.
You do not answer.

Days go by.
Weeks go by.
Months go by.
You reach out and ask me to meet you at a hotel.
It is clear you are trying to keep me a secret.
But I go along with it anyway.
Foolishly.

I meet up with you, and you leave soon after.
After having gotten what you came for.
You ignore me again, using your medication as an excuse.

Loved & Lost
You Will Always Be Remembered

I fall for it.

Days go by.
Weeks go by.
Months go by.
You reach out again.

I am excited.
You tell me you have met someone and are in a serious relationship.
Why would you tell me that?
Why would I want to hear that?
Why would I care?

Days go by.
Weeks go by.
Months go by.
Silence.

Loved & Lost
You Will Always Be Remembered

Write a letter expressing your true feelings to Mr. Wrong when you are trying to get over Mr. Right. What do you wish you could do differently? Do not suppress. Just write.

Loved & Lost
You Will Always Be Remembered

Draw an image representing the agony of what love looks like when it is completely wrong for you. Do not suppress. Just draw.

Loved & Lost
You Will Always Be Remembered

CHAPTER EIGHT

A Letter To The One Who Takes Advantage Of Me:
You Are The Reason I Remain Silent

My roommate said you raped me.
Did you?
I know we went out.
I know you bought me drinks.
Did you drug them?
What did you do to them?

Loved & Lost
You Will Always Be Remembered

What did you do to me?
I thought we were having a fun and casual date.
You show me your favorite bars, handing me drinks as I am distracted.
I should have known better.
But I am greedy for free cocktails, and I go along with it.

You introduce me to your friends and acquaintances, handing me drinks sporadically, as I sip on them, distracted.
Eight drinks later, I am in the bathroom, vomiting.
Crying.
Near death.

I quietly whisper, "I need help", but no one hears me.
I know, while throwing up, that you are trouble.
However, no one notices.
No one realizes I am in pain and danger.
Everyone assumes that I am another drunk college student.
Not a victim.

I get a cab.
You climb in with me.
No.
Get out.
But I am too weak and drunk to tell you so.

We go back to my dorm.
You put me in bed.
Tuck me in.

Loved & Lost
You Will Always Be Remembered

And instead of leaving, you climb in with me.
You undress me.
One item at a time.
Take advantage of me.

Hold my hair while I puke but continue to feel around.
Am I conscious?
Am I agreeing to this?
Am I giving you signs that I want this?
Was my roommate, right?
Did you rape me?

Loved & Lost
You Will Always Be Remembered

Write a letter expressing your true feelings to the one who takes advantage of you. What do you wish you could do differently? Do not suppress. Just write.

Loved & Lost
You Will Always Be Remembered

Draw an image representing the agony of what love feels like when you regret the choices you make. Do not suppress. Just draw.

Loved & Lost
You Will Always Be Remembered

CHAPTER NINE

A Letter To My Longest, Yet Most Toxic, Relationship:
You Are The Reason I Am Traumatized

You show up at my house, flowers in hand, charming as ever.
I am still in pain, so I fall for you immediately.
To this day, I still do not know whether I loved you.
We have an amazing first date and an amazing connection.
I want more.

Loved & Lost
You Will Always Be Remembered

I take two-hour bus rides to your apartment, a four-hour roundtrip.
I do not mind.
Then the fights begin.
One month into the relationship.

We argue, and you kick me out of your apartment, forcing me to stand outside in the dark, waiting for the next bus.
We fight, and you run off to other women for your emotional comfort instead of talking to me.
We both know our love is dysfunctional.
But we brush it off.

We pretend our toxic fights never happen.
And we love each other again.
For a week.
Then the cycle continues.

We love. We fight. We love again.
I then move in with you.
Six months in.
Against my better judgment.

We argue again, and you force me to move out.
I move into my own apartment.
I give you a call.
You say you still love me.
We get back together.

Loved & Lost
You Will Always Be Remembered

The cycle continues.
We love. We fight. We love again.
You then move in with me.
Against my better judgment.
We fight, and you move in with another woman.

I call you again.
You say you still love me.
We rent an apartment together and the fights get worse.
You hit me.
You refuse to pay rent.
You blame me for you losing your job.
What did I do?

Why am I still in this toxic relationship?
A toxic relationship consumed by physical abuse and infidelity.
I try leaving.
But I can't.
You move out.

I convince you to move back in.
Against my better judgment.
The cycle continues.
We love. We fight. We love again.

Then you ignore me.
Screaming at me for moving around in my own apartment.
You leave again.

Loved & Lost
You Will Always Be Remembered

This time I learn.
I stop calling.
I stop caring.
I stop loving.
You are my most toxic relationship.
And I am never going back.

Loved & Lost
You Will Always Be Remembered

Write a letter expressing your true feelings to the one who leaves you broken and abused. What do you wish you could do differently? Do not suppress. Just write.

Loved & Lost
You Will Always Be Remembered

Draw an image representing the agony of what it feels like to love someone who hurts you. Do not suppress. Just draw.

Loved & Lost
You Will Always Be Remembered

CHAPTER TEN

A Letter To The Unexpected And Shallow Breakup:
You Are The Reason I Despise Men

You are perfect.
In your fashionable suits and your stylish hats.
You laugh at all my jokes.
You listen to all my problems.
As inappropriate as they are.

We spend hours talking on the phone.

Loved & Lost
You Will Always Be Remembered

Our longest record is six.
I think.
I can't remember.
That's the longest time I have ever spoken to anyone.

You compliment me, and you seem genuinely happy to be with me.
But that is a lie.
Isn't it?

You never return my hints to take the relationship further.
You still talk to other women in hopes for a potential long-term partner.
I am not good enough.
Never for you.
Why are you with me then?
Why do you still come over if you do not see a future with me?

Then you call me up.
One month later.
You tell me it is over and that you have had doubts since week one.
The first week?
What the hell were you doing during the other three weeks?

We talk on the phone.
For hours.
You tell me I'm inconvenient.
I live less than an hour from you.

Loved & Lost
You Will Always Be Remembered

I cry in the middle of the street.

You only stay for as long as you do because you do not want to upset me.
Then you hang up.
And I am still in shock.
I smash all the gifts you have given me.
I regret opening my heart to you only to have it crushed so soon.

Our relationship seemed fine.
Perfect even.
Now it is over.
Just as quickly as it began.
You are the reason I begin writing.
So thank you.
But fuck you.

Two days later, I see pictures of you with someone else.
Good luck to her.
Fuck her.

Loved & Lost
You Will Always Be Remembered

Write a letter expressing your true feelings to the one who leaves you unexpectedly. What do you wish you could do differently? Do not suppress. Just write.

Loved & Lost
You Will Always Be Remembered

Draw an image representing the agony of what heartbreak feels like when you lose it on a whim. Do not suppress. Just draw.

Loved & Lost
You Will Always Be Remembered

CHAPTER ELEVEN

A Letter To The One I Left Unexpectedly:
You Are The Reason I Deserve To Be Ghosted

You did nothing wrong.
I'm sorry.
You are not at fault.
I am.

I find it difficult letting others down when I am not interested.
That is what I am doing to you.

Loved & Lost
You Will Always Be Remembered

I'm sorry.
I do not want to spend my life with someone who only talks about Jesus.

I cannot start a relationship with someone who already has kids.
I am shallow.
I know.
I should have been honest with you.
Instead of ghosting you.

I am making the wrong choice.
I turn down and hurt a perfect gentleman when all you want to do is watch a movie.
I still regret it.
I know you do not care.
But I still regret the impulsive actions I have made on my part.

I'm sorry.
You do not have to forgive me.
I do not expect you to forgive me.
You do not even need to know if I am sorry or not.
I'm just sorry.

Loved & Lost
You Will Always Be Remembered

Write a letter expressing your true feelings to the one you ghost. What do you wish you could do differently? Do not suppress. Just write.

Loved & Lost
You Will Always Be Remembered

Draw an image representing the agony of what goes through your mind when you choose to ghost someone. Do not suppress. Just draw.

Loved & Lost
You Will Always Be Remembered

CHAPTER TWELVE

A Letter To The One Who Could Have Been:
You Are The Reason I Have No Standards

Up until now, I thought I was alone in my witty sarcasm and terrible humor.
The first day I meet you, you take my breath away.
I feel like I can be myself around you, and I have the best first date of my life.
We connect so well, and sparks shoot everywhere.

Loved & Lost
You Will Always Be Remembered

However, there is one problem.
Not really.
Before we met, you told me you are not looking for anyone serious.
I choose to ignore that.
I see you as an amazing potential partner, and I do everything I can think of to get you to be with me.

I buy you gifts.
I give you space.
I share my feelings with you more times than I can count.
Every time we meet up, I feel like I never want the night to end.

You are perfect person for me, yet the perfect person I cannot have.
You keep telling me that we are not together.
I keep refusing to believe you.
We have great phone conversations, and you cheer me up every single time.

The more we talk, the more I see you as a boyfriend.
I ask you if you are dating anyone, and I pretend like I do not want you.
You tell me to mind my own business.
I continue to open my heart to you, sharing personal information and finding excuses to get closer to you.

You realize this.
I know you realize this.

Loved & Lost
You Will Always Be Remembered

Because you pull away the closer I come.
Every night I dream about you.
Wondering how my future would look with you in it.
I feel complete when I am around you.

When I am with you, there is not one dull moment.
But I am delusional.
You go from texting back once a day to once a week to once every three months.
Radio silence.

Then I see you with another woman.
Clearly in a relationship.
Nothing serious, my ass.

Loved & Lost
You Will Always Be Remembered

Write a letter expressing your true feelings to the one who refuses to love you back. What do you wish you could do differently? Do not suppress. Just write.

Loved & Lost
You Will Always Be Remembered

Draw an image representing the agony of your heart when your perfect relationship shatters. Do not suppress. Just draw.

Loved & Lost
You Will Always Be Remembered

CHAPTER THIRTEEN

**A Letter To The One Who Fell For All My Bullshit:
You Are The Reason I Have No Shame**

You are a nice person.
A great person.
I know that.
But I treat you like crap anyway.

Truth is, when we first met, I immediately knew I do not want to be with you.

Loved & Lost
You Will Always Be Remembered

But I continue to see you anyway.
As a distraction.
Out of boredom.

I make you drive over two hours to see me because I am bored.
I know.
I'm sorry.
But I do it again.
And again.

Every time I am bored.
I should have told you I am not interested sooner.
Rather than telling you, I ignore you instead, just like others have ignored me.
I string you along, and you fall for it.
I know.
I'm sorry.
But when I do tell you I am not interested, we argue, we fight, and I feel guilty.

A couple weeks go by.
I become bored again.
And I need another distraction.
I turn back to you because I know you will answer me.
You do.

We get back together.
I feel uneasy again.
I ignore you.

Loved & Lost
You Will Always Be Remembered

You realize it.
I continue making excuses to keep you around.

Our relationship always turns me off.
I tell you I am not seeing anyone else, but then I do.
I go back to you when it is convenient.
When I am lonely.

I know you see my flaws.
Yet, you stick around anyway.
While I turn to others.
I know.
I'm sorry.
But I will not change.

Loved & Lost
You Will Always Be Remembered

Write a letter expressing your true feelings to the one you use and abuse. What do you wish you could do differently? Do not suppress. Just write.

Loved & Lost
You Will Always Be Remembered

Draw an image representing the agony of what goes through your mind when you pretend to care for someone you do not. Do not suppress. Just draw.

Loved & Lost
You Will Always Be Remembered

CHAPTER FOURTEEN

A Letter To The One Who Refuses To Stop:
You Are The Reason I Fear Others

I know what you're thinking.
You're thinking that just because I ask you to sit next to me, it means I want to sleep with you.
No.
I am not.

Stop thinking that.

Loved & Lost
You Will Always Be Remembered

But that idea is already stuck in your head.
Isn't it?
I know because you invite yourself into my apartment and make your way inside of me.

I know because even when I push you away, you persist and hold me down.
I know because even when I tell you to leave, you continue to forcibly move your hands.
I freeze.
Traumatized.
Hoping the night will just end so I have an excuse to force you to leave.

I cry, and I hate the feeling of you touching me.
I pray this moment ends because I feel disgusting and abused.
I just want you to go.
Please stop.
I beg you.
Just stop.
I don't want to do this.

Why did I let you in?
Why didn't I call the cops?
Oh god.
Please just stop!

The morning comes.
I cry with joy.

Loved & Lost
You Will Always Be Remembered

I get up and tell you to leave so I can go to work.
I lock myself in the bathroom for an hour.
I come out.
You're still here.
Smoking a joint when you are clearly inexperienced.

I tell you to leave now.
You resist.
I repeat myself.
This time, louder and angrier.

You finally leave, with hopes that you will see me again.
I do not correct you.
You text me hours later.
I block you.

Loved & Lost
You Will Always Be Remembered

Write a letter expressing your true feelings to the one you wish to forget. What do you wish you could do differently? Do not suppress. Just write.

Loved & Lost
You Will Always Be Remembered

Draw an image representing the agony when it feels like you cannot get away. Do not suppress. Just draw.

Loved & Lost
You Will Always Be Remembered

CHAPTER FIFTEEN

A Letter To The One Who Ghosted Me:
I Deserve It.
Karma Does Exist.

You saw my crazy early on.
Or at least, the lower spectrum of it.
You are one of those people.
What do you call them?
The "ghosters".

Loved & Lost
You Will Always Be Remembered

I knew you did not like me after the way our first date ended.
Why don't you just tell me?
Instead of making me reach out to you.
Coming off as insane and crazy.

I really tried with you.
I quell my crazy behaviors, and I wait for you, patiently.
However, you continue to ignore me.
Using the excuse that you do not have to respond to my texts "immediately".
Texting back "immediately" means within a few seconds.
Not within a few weeks.

I thought we had a great time.
I send you my stories.
I wish you luck on your workshop.
I support your career even though I think it is stupid.
But you still ignore me.

You then let me know that you will reach out "soon".
I get my hopes up.
That was nine months ago.
What is your definition of "soon"?
Good luck with your acting career.
You are a great liar.

Loved & Lost
You Will Always Be Remembered

Write a letter expressing your true feelings to the one who ghosts you. What do you wish you could do differently? Do not suppress. Just write.

Loved & Lost
You Will Always Be Remembered

Draw an image representing the agony of how you feel when someone does not stay but does not leave. Do not suppress. Just draw.

Loved & Lost
You Will Always Be Remembered

CHAPTER SIXTEEN

**A Letter To The One Who Calls Me A Freak For Being Myself:
You Are The Reason I Pretend To Be Someone I'm Not**

I meet up with you.
You're nothing special.
Just someone I needed to distract myself from my problems.
I do not need you.

But you don't know that.
I need you to need me.

Loved & Lost
You Will Always Be Remembered

But not the other way around.

We go out.
I don't know what I'm doing.
I just pretend I do.
To impress you.
Why?

I have no idea.
I just want you to stick around.
I don't even like you.
But you don't know that.

We come back.
I thought the date went horribly.
I still don't like you.
But you don't know that.
You still seem to like me.
So, I just go with it.

You make a move.
I still don't like you.
But I do not stop you.
I let it go.
I miss the attention.
I crave human touch.

I become vulnerable even when my feelings are only disgust.
I let it go.

Loved & Lost
You Will Always Be Remembered

I get my attention.
You get what you want.
You get off.
And then you leave.

The next morning, you become angry that I had made plans that do not involve you.
You hate that I do not put you first.
You hate that you are not getting what you want all the time.

You become resentful.
You manifest your anger onto me.
You call me a "freak", as well as many other insults.

You end the conversation by blocking me before I even have the chance to look at my phone.
I brush it off.
I don't care.
I don't like you.
I never liked you.
But you will never know that.

Loved & Lost
You Will Always Be Remembered

Write a letter expressing your true feelings to the one you open up to because you crave love and attention. What do you wish you could do differently? Do not suppress. Just write.

Loved & Lost
You Will Always Be Remembered

Draw an image representing the agony of how it feels to give yourself to someone you despise. Do not suppress. Just draw.

Loved & Lost
You Will Always Be Remembered

CHAPTER SEVENTEEN

A Letter To The One Who Lured Me In With No Intention Of Keeping Me:
You Are The Reason I Question My Judgments

You have everything.
Looks.
Charm.
Humor.
Career.
Life.

Loved & Lost
You Will Always Be Remembered

While I am still a simpleton looking for love.

You find me lovely.
You find me quirky.
You see me as a potential partner.
Or that's what I thought.
No.

Now I know.
You only saw me as another fling.
To get what you want.
Then to throw me out.

You thought I was stupid.
You thought I was too naïve to know what was going on.
You were right.
I was naïve.
I was so desperate to find love that I could not see the reality of the situation.

We start off innocent.
Coffee.
Board games.
Music.

Then it becomes awkward.
Then you change.
The monster comes out.
I no longer recognize you.

Loved & Lost
You Will Always Be Remembered

The person I have known for two days.
Now becomes someone seeking lust, and lust alone.

What happened?
Why did I agree to go along with this?
What is wrong with me?
Why did I travel three hours just to be used?
Then it stops.

You get up.
Escort me out of your apartment.
And I never hear from you again.

Loved & Lost
You Will Always Be Remembered

Write a letter expressing your true feelings to someone innocent turned monster. What do you wish you could do differently? Do not suppress. Just write.

Loved & Lost
You Will Always Be Remembered

Draw an image representing the agony of what the monster inside of you looks like. Do not suppress. Just draw.

Loved & Lost
You Will Always Be Remembered

CHAPTER EIGHTEEN

**A Letter To The One Who Thinks I Will Never Be Good Enough:
You Are The Reason I Turn Against Myself**

You're old.
You're ugly.
You're shallow.
I can never see myself with you.
I can never like you.

So, why am I still texting you?

Loved & Lost
You Will Always Be Remembered

Why am I still sending flirts and images back and forth?
Why am I still letting arguments with you tear me apart?
Why am I still hoping that you will love me?
Why am I still talking to you?

I should have let you go when you first decided to ignore me.
I should have let you go when I knew this isn't going anywhere.
I should have let you go when you first asked me to do things that were against my beliefs.
I should have let you go when I knew I am never going to love you.
I should have let you go when I saw you.

Why did I persist?
Was it because of loneliness?
Was it because I knew you were interested so I tried holding onto that?
Was it because I thought I would regret it if I let you go?
Was it because I thought I couldn't do better?
Was it because I just wanted someone to love me?

Never have I ever felt so controlled by someone I didn't even like.
Never have I ever thought I would surrender everything I am for everything I'm not.
Never have I ever thought I would completely lose myself for a man.
Never have I ever thought I would get out of the mess you had pulled me in.

Loved & Lost
You Will Always Be Remembered

But I did.
So, take your flirts and your images, and guilt-trip someone else with unwanted solicitations.

Loved & Lost
You Will Always Be Remembered

Write a letter expressing your true feelings to the one who turns you against your better judgment. What do you wish you could do differently? Do not suppress. Just write.

Loved & Lost
You Will Always Be Remembered

Draw an image representing the agony of what it looks like when you completely lose sense of who you are. Do not suppress. Just draw.

Loved & Lost
You Will Always Be Remembered

CHAPTER NINETEEN

A Letter To The Love I Have Found:
Will You Leave Too?
Or Will My Pattern Of Unfortunate Relationships Finally Come To An End?

When I met you, I had no idea what I wanted.
I almost didn't show up.
I was not at a place where I cared enough to try.

But I show up anyway.

Loved & Lost
You Will Always Be Remembered

And there you are.
Quiet.
Mysterious.
Different.

The night starts off as the other nights.
Uncomfortable.
New.
Awkward.
Silent.

But then something changes.
As if some power overcame me.
And I share with you everything.
My flaws.
My traumas.
My insecurities.
My past.
And you do not run away.

Surprising.
That's a first.
Soon, we become closer.
Sharing every part of our lives with each other.
We see each other as potential partners.

You see no faults in me.
You're different.
You stay.

Loved & Lost
You Will Always Be Remembered

Not out of obligation.
Not out of desperation.
But out of love.

That's different.
That's pressure.
That's scary.

I hope I don't mess it up.
I'll probably mess it up.
My track record.
I'm a mess.

But you hold on.
You stay.
Even when I do mess up.
Is that true love?
Am I capable of true love?

I may never know the answer.
I guess we shall see.
Where our journey takes us.
I guess we shall see.
Whether you end up only in my memories.
I love you.

Loved & Lost
You Will Always Be Remembered

Write a letter expressing your true feelings to the one you currently love. What do you wish you could do differently? Do not suppress. Just write.

Loved & Lost
You Will Always Be Remembered

Draw an image representing the agony of your current romantic situation. Do not suppress. Just draw.

Loved & Lost
You Will Always Be Remembered

CHAPTER TWENTY

A Letter To The Person I Have Neglected My Entire Life:
You Are My One True Love, And I Will Never Leave You Again

I have pushed you aside my entire life.
Always choosing men and obsessive love over you.
I'm sorry.

I have hurt you and insulted you, in hopes that I would obtain
potential love.
I'm sorry.

Loved & Lost
You Will Always Be Remembered

I have forced you into situations that have made you cry and have turned my back on you when all you wanted was a hug.
I'm sorry.

I have hated you for making me choose and lied to you for making me wait.
I'm sorry.

I'm sorry for putting you in situations that made you hate yourself.
I'm sorry for forcing you to go against your beliefs which have made you hurt yourself.
I'm sorry for all the words I have said when I thought I meant them.
I'm sorry for always putting you last while my desperation first.
I'm sorry.

Will you ever forgive me?
Will you ever let me back in?
Will you ever trust me again?
After all I have put you through?
Will you ever love me again?
Have you ever loved me?

Do I still have a chance?
Or is it time to let go?
Have my actions been so drastic that there is no turning back?
I want to love you again.

Loved & Lost
You Will Always Be Remembered

I want to be there for you through thick and thin.
I want to never let another boy, or another man, come between you and me.

I want to show you that you do not deserve neglect and hatred, despite how much you were shown before.
I want to show you that you are worthy of being loved.
I want to love you.
Please love me back.

Loved & Lost
You Will Always Be Remembered

Write a letter expressing your true feelings to the self you have neglected during your search for potential love. What do you wish you could do differently? Do not suppress. Just write.

Loved & Lost
You Will Always Be Remembered

Draw an image representing the beauty of what it means to truly love yourself. Do not suppress. Just draw.

Loved & Lost
You Will Always Be Remembered

EPILOGUE

Emotions are powerful.
Emotions make us feel as if we are engaging in actions we cannot control.
Emotions make us impulsively react to situations that we later regret.

Emotions make us become desperate when it comes to finding love and when we are losing love.
Emotions can make us become crazy.
We turn into tears.

Loved & Lost
You Will Always Be Remembered

We turn into fury.
We turn into resentment, where we are only focused on two things.
Revenge.
And new love.

Our emotions become so strong that, instead of turning inward when a relationship ends, we remain outward.
We jump from potential partner to potential partner because our emotions desperately make us find replacements rather than learn to love ourselves.
We believe we are massively flawed when our love is not returned.

We fail to see that the opinions of others do not define our worth.
And that our opinions of ourselves are the only ones that do.
We need to reframe our emotions and stop using them to define our personalities and actions.
We need to discover who we are outside of unrequited and destructive love, and realize that we do not have to be destroyed by them.

Can we finally learn that love does not control us after all?
Can we finally learn that love is only defined by the emotions we feed into it?
Or will we perish once again the next time someone buys us a ring and takes it away?
Do not perish.

Loved & Lost
You Will Always Be Remembered

Loved & Lost
You Will Always Be Remembered

LOVE LETTER

Not easy to state the change you made.
If I'm alive now, then I was dead,
Though, like a stone, unbothered by it,
Staying put according to habit.
You didn't just tow me an inch, no--
Nor leave me to set my small bald eye
Skyward again, without hope, of course,
Of apprehending blueness, or stars.

That wasn't it. I slept, say: a snake
Masked among black rocks as a black rock
In the white hiatus of winter--
Like my neighbors, taking no pleasure
In the million perfectly-chisled
Cheeks alighting each moment to melt
My cheeks of basalt. They turned to tears,
Angels weeping over dull natures,
But didn't convince me. Those tears froze.
Each dead head had a visor of ice.
And I slept on like a bent finger.
The first thing I was was sheer air
And the locked drops rising in dew

Loved & Lost
You Will Always Be Remembered

Limpid as spirits. Many stones lay
Dense and expressionless round about.
I didn't know what to make of it.
I shone, mice-scaled, and unfolded
To pour myself out like a fluid
Among bird feet and the stems of plants.
I wasn't fooled. I knew you at once.

Tree and stone glittered, without shadows.
My finger-length grew lucent as glass.
I started to bud like a March twig:
An arm and a leg, and arm, a leg.
From stone to cloud, so I ascended.
Now I resemble a sort of god
Floating through the air in my soul-shift
Pure as a pane of ice. It's a gift.

- Sylvia Plath

Loved & Lost
You Will Always Be Remembered

An acknowledgment to all my past relationships and potential loves. I hope one day you are also able to escape the perils of your emotions.

Loved & Lost
You Will Always Be Remembered

Loved & Lost
You Will Always Be Remembered

Loved & Lost
You Will Always Be Remembered

www.ingramcontent.com/pod-product-compliance
Lightning Source LLC
Chambersburg PA
CBHW070952080526
44587CB00015B/2281